Fishing Logbook

Logbook #	
Book Continued From #	
Book Continued To #	
Date Book Started	
Date Book Ended	
Name	
Address	
Phone Number	
Email	

Notes

Fishing Log

Location: _____ Date: _____

Location Details: _____

_____

Companions: _____

Water Temp: _____ Air Temp: _____ Hours Fished: _____

Wind Direction: _____ Wind Speed: _____ Humidity: _____

Weather: ☀ ☁ ☔ ❄ _____

Moon Phase: _____ ◐ ◑ ● ◐ ◑ ○

Tide Details: _____

Notes: _____

_____

Fish Caught

Species	Bait	Length	Weight	Time
Other Notes:				
Other Notes:				
Other Notes:				
Other Notes:				
Other Notes:				
Other Notes:				
Other Notes:				
Other Notes:				

Fish Caught

Species	Bait	Length	Weight	Time
Other Notes:				
Other Notes:				
Other Notes:				
Other Notes:				
Other Notes:				
Other Notes:				
Other Notes:				
Other Notes:				
Other Notes:				

Other Important Notes:

_____

_____

_____

_____

_____

_____

_____

_____

Rating Your Experience: _____ ☆ ☆ ☆ ☆ ☆

Fishing Log

Location: _____ Date: _____

Location Details: _____

_____

Companions: _____

Water Temp: _____ Air Temp: _____ Hours Fished: _____

Wind Direction: _____ Wind Speed: _____ Humidity: _____

Weather: ☀ ☁ 🌧 ❄ _____

Moon Phase: _____ ◐ ◑ ● ◑ ◐ ○

Tide Details: _____

Notes: _____

_____

Fish Caught

Species	Bait	Length	Weight	Time
Other Notes:				
Other Notes:				
Other Notes:				
Other Notes:				
Other Notes:				
Other Notes:				
Other Notes:				
Other Notes:				

Fish Caught

Species	Bait	Length	Weight	Time
Other Notes:				
Other Notes:				
Other Notes:				
Other Notes:				
Other Notes:				
Other Notes:				
Other Notes:				
Other Notes:				
Other Notes:				

Other Important Notes:

_____

_____

_____

_____

_____

_____

_____

_____

Rating Your Experience: _____ ☆ ☆ ☆ ☆ ☆

Fishing Log

Location: _____ Date: _____

Location Details: _____

_____

Companions: _____

Water Temp: _____ Air Temp: _____ Hours Fished: _____

Wind Direction: _____ Wind Speed: _____ Humidity: _____

Weather: ☀ ☁ ⛆ ❄ _____

Moon Phase: _____ ☽ ☽ ● ☾ ☾ ○

Tide Details: _____

Notes: _____

_____

Fish Caught

Species	Bait	Length	Weight	Time
Other Notes:				
Other Notes:				
Other Notes:				
Other Notes:				
Other Notes:				
Other Notes:				
Other Notes:				
Other Notes:				

Fish Caught

Species	Bait	Length	Weight	Time
Other Notes:				
Other Notes:				
Other Notes:				
Other Notes:				
Other Notes:				
Other Notes:				
Other Notes:				
Other Notes:				
Other Notes:				

Other Important Notes:

_____

_____

_____

_____

_____

_____

_____

_____

Rating Your Experience: _____ ☆ ☆ ☆ ☆ ☆

Fishing Log

Location: _____ Date: _____

Location Details: _____

_____

Companions: _____

Water Temp: _____ Air Temp: _____ Hours Fished: _____

Wind Direction: _____ Wind Speed: _____ Humidity: _____

Weather: ☀ ☁ ☂ ❄ _____

Moon Phase: _____ ◗ ◖ ● ◗ ◖ ○

Tide Details: _____

Notes: _____

_____

Fish Caught

Species	Bait	Length	Weight	Time
Other Notes:				
Other Notes:				
Other Notes:				
Other Notes:				
Other Notes:				
Other Notes:				
Other Notes:				
Other Notes:				

Fish Caught

Species	Bait	Length	Weight	Time
Other Notes:				
Other Notes:				
Other Notes:				
Other Notes:				
Other Notes:				
Other Notes:				
Other Notes:				
Other Notes:				
Other Notes:				

Other Important Notes:

_____

_____

_____

_____

_____

_____

_____

_____

Rating Your Experience: _ _____ ☆ ☆ ☆ ☆ ☆

Fishing Log

Location: _____ Date: _____

Location Details: _____

_____

Companions: _____

Water Temp: _____ Air Temp: _____ Hours Fished: _____

Wind Direction: _____ Wind Speed: _____ Humidity: _____

Weather: ☀ ☁ ☔ ❄ _____

Moon Phase: _____ ◗ ◑ ● ◐ ◑ ◯

Tide Details: _____

Notes: _____

_____

Fish Caught

Species	Bait	Length	Weight	Time
Other Notes:				
Other Notes:				
Other Notes:				
Other Notes:				
Other Notes:				
Other Notes:				
Other Notes:				
Other Notes:				

Fish Caught

Species	Bait	Length	Weight	Time
Other Notes:				
Other Notes:				
Other Notes:				
Other Notes:				
Other Notes:				
Other Notes:				
Other Notes:				
Other Notes:				
Other Notes:				

Other Important Notes:

_____

_____

_____

_____

_____

_____

_____

_____

Rating Your Experience: _____ ☆ ☆ ☆ ☆ ☆

Fishing Log

Location: _____ Date: _____

Location Details: _____
_____

Companions: _____

Water Temp: _____ Air Temp: _____ Hours Fished: _____

Wind Direction: _____ Wind Speed: _____ Humidity: _____

Weather: ☀ ☁ ☔ ❄ _____

Moon Phase: _____ ◖ ◗ ● ◑ ◔ ○

Tide Details: _____

Notes: _____

_____

Fish Caught

Species	Bait	Length	Weight	Time
Other Notes:				
Other Notes:				
Other Notes:				
Other Notes:				
Other Notes:				
Other Notes:				
Other Notes:				
Other Notes:				

Fish Caught

Species	Bait	Length	Weight	Time
Other Notes:				
Other Notes:				
Other Notes:				
Other Notes:				
Other Notes:				
Other Notes:				
Other Notes:				
Other Notes:				
Other Notes:				

Other Important Notes:

_____

_____

_____

_____

_____

_____

_____

_____

Rating Your Experience: _ _____ ☆ ☆ ☆ ☆ ☆

Fishing Log

Location: _____ Date: _____

Location Details: _____

_____

Companions: _____

Water Temp: _____ Air Temp: _____ Hours Fished: _____

Wind Direction: _____ Wind Speed: _____ Humidity: _____

Weather: ☀ ☁ 🌧 🌨 _____

Moon Phase: _____ 🌒 🌓 🌑 🌗 🌘 🌕

Tide Details: _____

Notes: _____

_____

Fish Caught

Species	Bait	Length	Weight	Time
Other Notes:				
Other Notes:				
Other Notes:				
Other Notes:				
Other Notes:				
Other Notes:				
Other Notes:				
Other Notes:				

Fish Caught

Species	Bait	Length	Weight	Time
Other Notes:				
Other Notes:				
Other Notes:				
Other Notes:				
Other Notes:				
Other Notes:				
Other Notes:				
Other Notes:				
Other Notes:				

Other Important Notes:

_____

_____

_____

_____

_____

_____

_____

_____

Rating Your Experience: _____ ☆ ☆ ☆ ☆ ☆

Fishing Log

Location: _____ Date: _____

Location Details: _____

_____

Companions: _____

Water Temp: _____ Air Temp: _____ Hours Fished: _____

Wind Direction: _____ Wind Speed: _____ Humidity: _____

Weather: ☀ ☁ ☔ ❄ _____

Moon Phase: _____ ◑ ◑ ● ◐ ◐ ○

Tide Details: _____

Notes: _____

_____

Fish Caught

Species	Bait	Length	Weight	Time
Other Notes:				
Other Notes:				
Other Notes:				
Other Notes:				
Other Notes:				
Other Notes:				
Other Notes:				
Other Notes:				

Fish Caught

Species	Bait	Length	Weight	Time
Other Notes:				
Other Notes:				
Other Notes:				
Other Notes:				
Other Notes:				
Other Notes:				
Other Notes:				
Other Notes:				
Other Notes:				

Other Important Notes:

_____

_____

_____

_____

_____

_____

_____

_____

Rating Your Experience: _____ ☆ ☆ ☆ ☆ ☆

Fishing Log

Location: _____ Date: _____

Location Details: _____

_____

Companions: _____

Water Temp: _____ Air Temp: _____ Hours Fished: _____

Wind Direction: _____ Wind Speed: _____ Humidity: _____

Weather: ☀ ☁ ☂ ❄ _____

Moon Phase: _____ ◐ ◑ ● ◑ ◐ ○

Tide Details: _____

Notes: _____

_____

Fish Caught

Species	Bait	Length	Weight	Time
Other Notes:				
Other Notes:				
Other Notes:				
Other Notes:				
Other Notes:				
Other Notes:				
Other Notes:				
Other Notes:				

Fish Caught

Species	Bait	Length	Weight	Time
Other Notes:				
Other Notes:				
Other Notes:				
Other Notes:				
Other Notes:				
Other Notes:				
Other Notes:				
Other Notes:				
Other Notes:				

Other Important Notes:

_____

_____

_____

_____

_____

_____

_____

_____

Rating Your Experience: _____ ☆ ☆ ☆ ☆ ☆

Fishing Log

Location: _____ Date: _____

Location Details: _____

_____

Companions: _____

Water Temp: _____ Air Temp: _____ Hours Fished: _____

Wind Direction: _____ Wind Speed: _____ Humidity: _____

Weather: ☀ ☁ ☂ ❄ _____

Moon Phase: _____ ◑ ◐ ● ◐ ◑ ○

Tide Details: _____

Notes: _____

_____

Fish Caught

Species	Bait	Length	Weight	Time
Other Notes:				
Other Notes:				
Other Notes:				
Other Notes:				
Other Notes:				
Other Notes:				
Other Notes:				
Other Notes:				

Fish Caught

Species	Bait	Length	Weight	Time
Other Notes:				
Other Notes:				
Other Notes:				
Other Notes:				
Other Notes:				
Other Notes:				
Other Notes:				
Other Notes:				
Other Notes:				

Other Important Notes:

_____

_____

_____

_____

_____

_____

_____

_____

Rating Your Experience: _____ ☆ ☆ ☆ ☆ ☆

Fishing Log

Location: _____ Date: _____

Location Details: _____

_____

Companions: _____

Water Temp: _____ Air Temp: _____ Hours Fished: _____

Wind Direction: _____ Wind Speed: _____ Humidity: _____

Weather: ☀ ☁ ⛅ ❄ _____

Moon Phase: _____ ◗ ◖ ● ◐ ◑ ○

Tide Details: _____

Notes: _____

_____

Fish Caught

Species	Bait	Length	Weight	Time
Other Notes:				
Other Notes:				
Other Notes:				
Other Notes:				
Other Notes:				
Other Notes:				
Other Notes:				
Other Notes:				

Fish Caught

Species	Bait	Length	Weight	Time
Other Notes:				
Other Notes:				
Other Notes:				
Other Notes:				
Other Notes:				
Other Notes:				
Other Notes:				
Other Notes:				
Other Notes:				

Other Important Notes:

_____

_____

_____

_____

_____

_____

_____

_____

Rating Your Experience: _____ ☆ ☆ ☆ ☆ ☆

Fishing Log

Location: _____ Date: _____

Location Details: _____

_____

Companions: _____

Water Temp: _____ Air Temp: _____ Hours Fished: _____

Wind Direction: _____ Wind Speed: _____ Humidity: _____

Weather: ☀ ☁ ⛆ ❄ _____

Moon Phase: _____ ◑ ◑ ● ◐ ◐ ○

Tide Details: _____

Notes: _____

_____

Fish Caught

Species	Bait	Length	Weight	Time
Other Notes:				
Other Notes:				
Other Notes:				
Other Notes:				
Other Notes:				
Other Notes:				
Other Notes:				
Other Notes:				

Fish Caught

Species	Bait	Length	Weight	Time
Other Notes:				
Other Notes:				
Other Notes:				
Other Notes:				
Other Notes:				
Other Notes:				
Other Notes:				
Other Notes:				
Other Notes:				

Other Important Notes:

_____

_____

_____

_____

_____

_____

_____

_____

Rating Your Experience: _____ ☆ ☆ ☆ ☆ ☆

Fishing Log

Location: _____ Date: _____

Location Details: _____

_____

Companions: _____

Water Temp: _____ Air Temp: _____ Hours Fished: _____

Wind Direction: _____ Wind Speed: _____ Humidity: _____

Weather: ☀ ☁ 🌧 ❄ _____

Moon Phase: _____ ◐ ◑ ● ◑ ◐ ○

Tide Details: _____

Notes: _____

_____

Fish Caught

Species	Bait	Length	Weight	Time
Other Notes:				
Other Notes:				
Other Notes:				
Other Notes:				
Other Notes:				
Other Notes:				
Other Notes:				
Other Notes:				

Fish Caught

Species	Bait	Length	Weight	Time
Other Notes:				
Other Notes:				
Other Notes:				
Other Notes:				
Other Notes:				
Other Notes:				
Other Notes:				
Other Notes:				
Other Notes:				

Other Important Notes:

_____

_____

_____

_____

_____

_____

_____

_____

Rating Your Experience: _____ ☆ ☆ ☆ ☆ ☆

Fishing Log

Location: _____ Date: _____

Location Details: _____

_____

Companions: _____

Water Temp: _____ Air Temp: _____ Hours Fished: _____

Wind Direction: _____ Wind Speed: _____ Humidity: _____

Weather: ☀ ☁ ☇ ❄ _____

Moon Phase: _____ ◗ ◑ ● ◐ ◐ ○

Tide Details: _____

Notes: _____

_____

Fish Caught

Species	Bait	Length	Weight	Time
Other Notes:				
Other Notes:				
Other Notes:				
Other Notes:				
Other Notes:				
Other Notes:				
Other Notes:				
Other Notes:				

Fish Caught

Species	Bait	Length	Weight	Time
Other Notes:				
Other Notes:				
Other Notes:				
Other Notes:				
Other Notes:				
Other Notes:				
Other Notes:				
Other Notes:				
Other Notes:				

Other Important Notes:

_____

_____

_____

_____

_____

_____

_____

_____

_____

Rating Your Experience: _____ ☆ ☆ ☆ ☆ ☆

Fishing Log

Location: _____ Date: _____

Location Details: _____

_____

Companions: _____

Water Temp: _____ Air Temp: _____ Hours Fished: _____

Wind Direction: _____ Wind Speed: _____ Humidity: _____

Weather: ☀ ☁ ☔ ❄ _____

Moon Phase: _____ ◑ ◑ ● ◐ ◐ ○

Tide Details: _____

Notes: _____

_____

Fish Caught

Species	Bait	Length	Weight	Time
Other Notes:				
Other Notes:				
Other Notes:				
Other Notes:				
Other Notes:				
Other Notes:				
Other Notes:				
Other Notes:				

Fish Caught

Species	Bait	Length	Weight	Time
Other Notes:				
Other Notes:				
Other Notes:				
Other Notes:				
Other Notes:				
Other Notes:				
Other Notes:				
Other Notes:				
Other Notes:				

Other Important Notes:

_____

_____

_____

_____

_____

_____

_____

_____

Rating Your Experience: _____ ☆ ☆ ☆ ☆ ☆

Fishing Log

Location: _____ Date: _____

Location Details: _____

_____

Companions: _____

Water Temp: _____ Air Temp: _____ Hours Fished: _____

Wind Direction: _____ Wind Speed: _____ Humidity: _____

Weather: ☀ ☁ ☔ ❄ _____

Moon Phase: _____ ◐ ◑ ● ◑ ◐ ○

Tide Details: _____

Notes: _____

_____

Fish Caught

Species	Bait	Length	Weight	Time
Other Notes:				
Other Notes:				
Other Notes:				
Other Notes:				
Other Notes:				
Other Notes:				
Other Notes:				
Other Notes:				

Fish Caught

Species	Bait	Length	Weight	Time
Other Notes:				
Other Notes:				
Other Notes:				
Other Notes:				
Other Notes:				
Other Notes:				
Other Notes:				
Other Notes:				
Other Notes:				

Other Important Notes:

_____

_____

_____

_____

_____

_____

_____

_____

Rating Your Experience: _____ ☆ ☆ ☆ ☆ ☆

Fishing Log

Location: _____   Date: _____

Location Details: _____

_____

Companions: _____

Water Temp: _____   Air Temp: _____   Hours Fished: _____

Wind Direction: _____   Wind Speed: _____   Humidity: _____

Weather: ☀ ☁ ☔ ❄ _____

Moon Phase: _____   ◐ ◑ ● ◑ ◐ ○

Tide Details: _____

Notes: _____

_____

Fish Caught

Species	Bait	Length	Weight	Time
Other Notes:				
Other Notes:				
Other Notes:				
Other Notes:				
Other Notes:				
Other Notes:				
Other Notes:				
Other Notes:				

Fish Caught

Species	Bait	Length	Weight	Time
Other Notes:				
Other Notes:				
Other Notes:				
Other Notes:				
Other Notes:				
Other Notes:				
Other Notes:				
Other Notes:				
Other Notes:				

Other Important Notes:

_____

_____

_____

_____

_____

_____

_____

_____

Rating Your Experience: _ _____ ☆ ☆ ☆ ☆ ☆

Fishing Log

Location: _____ Date: _____

Location Details: _____

_____

Companions: _____

Water Temp: _____ Air Temp: _____ Hours Fished: _____

Wind Direction: _____ Wind Speed: _____ Humidity: _____

Weather: ☀ ☁ 🌧 ❄ _____

Moon Phase: _____ ◗ ◑ ● ◐ ◐ ○

Tide Details: _____

Notes: _____

_____

Fish Caught

Species	Bait	Length	Weight	Time
Other Notes:				
Other Notes:				
Other Notes:				
Other Notes:				
Other Notes:				
Other Notes:				
Other Notes:				
Other Notes:				

Fish Caught

Species	Bait	Length	Weight	Time
Other Notes:				
Other Notes:				
Other Notes:				
Other Notes:				
Other Notes:				
Other Notes:				
Other Notes:				
Other Notes:				
Other Notes:				

Other Important Notes:

_____

_____

_____

_____

_____

_____

_____

_____

Rating Your Experience: _____ ☆ ☆ ☆ ☆ ☆

Fishing Log

Location: _____ Date: _____

Location Details: _____

_____

Companions: _____

Water Temp: _____ Air Temp: _____ Hours Fished: _____

Wind Direction: _____ Wind Speed: _____ Humidity: _____

Weather: ☀ ☁ ☂ ❄ _____

Moon Phase: _____ ◐ ◑ ● ◑ ◐ ○

Tide Details: _____

Notes: _____

_____

Fish Caught

Species	Bait	Length	Weight	Time
Other Notes:				
Other Notes:				
Other Notes:				
Other Notes:				
Other Notes:				
Other Notes:				
Other Notes:				
Other Notes:				

Fish Caught

Species	Bait	Length	Weight	Time
Other Notes:				
Other Notes:				
Other Notes:				
Other Notes:				
Other Notes:				
Other Notes:				
Other Notes:				
Other Notes:				
Other Notes:				

Other Important Notes:

_____

_____

_____

_____

_____

_____

_____

_____

Rating Your Experience: _____ ☆ ☆ ☆ ☆ ☆

Fishing Log

Location: _____ Date: _____

Location Details: _____

_____

Companions: _____

Water Temp: _____ Air Temp: _____ Hours Fished: _____

Wind Direction: _____ Wind Speed: _____ Humidity: _____

Weather: ☀ ☁ 🌧 ❄ _____

Moon Phase: _____ ◑ ◑ ● ◑ ◐ ○

Tide Details: _____

Notes: _____

_____

Fish Caught

Species	Bait	Length	Weight	Time
Other Notes:				
Other Notes:				
Other Notes:				
Other Notes:				
Other Notes:				
Other Notes:				
Other Notes:				
Other Notes:				

Fish Caught

Species	Bait	Length	Weight	Time
Other Notes:				
Other Notes:				
Other Notes:				
Other Notes:				
Other Notes:				
Other Notes:				
Other Notes:				
Other Notes:				
Other Notes:				

Other Important Notes:

_____

_____

_____

_____

_____

_____

_____

_____

Rating Your Experience: _____ ☆ ☆ ☆ ☆ ☆

Fishing Log

Location: _____ Date: _____

Location Details: _____

_____

Companions: _____

Water Temp: _____ Air Temp: _____ Hours Fished: _____

Wind Direction: _____ Wind Speed: _____ Humidity: _____

Weather: ☀ ☁ ☔ ❄ _____

Moon Phase: _____ 🌑🌓🌕🌗🌑🌕

Tide Details: _____

Notes: _____

_____

Fish Caught

Species	Bait	Length	Weight	Time
Other Notes:				
Other Notes:				
Other Notes:				
Other Notes:				
Other Notes:				
Other Notes:				
Other Notes:				
Other Notes:				

Fish Caught

Species	Bait	Length	Weight	Time
Other Notes:				
Other Notes:				
Other Notes:				
Other Notes:				
Other Notes:				
Other Notes:				
Other Notes:				
Other Notes:				
Other Notes:				

Other Important Notes:

_____

_____

_____

_____

_____

_____

_____

_____

Rating Your Experience: _____ ☆ ☆ ☆ ☆ ☆

Fishing Log

Location: _____ Date: _____

Location Details: _____

_____

Companions: _____

Water Temp: _____ Air Temp: _____ Hours Fished: _____

Wind Direction: _____ Wind Speed: _____ Humidity: _____

Weather: ☀ ☁ ☔ ❄ _____

Moon Phase: _____ ◗ ◗ ● ◖ ◖ ○

Tide Details: _____

Notes: _____

Fish Caught

Species	Bait	Length	Weight	Time
Other Notes:				
Other Notes:				
Other Notes:				
Other Notes:				
Other Notes:				
Other Notes:				
Other Notes:				
Other Notes:				

Fish Caught

Species	Bait	Length	Weight	Time
Other Notes:				
Other Notes:				
Other Notes:				
Other Notes:				
Other Notes:				
Other Notes:				
Other Notes:				
Other Notes:				
Other Notes:				

Other Important Notes:

_____

_____

_____

_____

_____

_____

_____

_____

Rating Your Experience: _____ ☆ ☆ ☆ ☆ ☆

Fishing Log

Location: _____ Date: _____

Location Details: _____

_____

Companions: _____

Water Temp: _____ Air Temp: _____ Hours Fished: _____

Wind Direction: _____ Wind Speed: _____ Humidity: _____

Weather: ☀ ☁ ☔ ❄ _____

Moon Phase: _____ ◐ ◑ ● ◑ ◐ ○

Tide Details: _____

Notes: _____

_____

Fish Caught

Species	Bait	Length	Weight	Time
Other Notes:				
Other Notes:				
Other Notes:				
Other Notes:				
Other Notes:				
Other Notes:				
Other Notes:				
Other Notes:				

Fish Caught

Species	Bait	Length	Weight	Time
Other Notes:				
Other Notes:				
Other Notes:				
Other Notes:				
Other Notes:				
Other Notes:				
Other Notes:				
Other Notes:				
Other Notes:				

Other Important Notes:

_____

_____

_____

_____

_____

_____

_____

_____

Rating Your Experience: _____ ☆ ☆ ☆ ☆ ☆

Fishing Log

Location: _____ Date: _____

Location Details: _____

_____

Companions: _____

Water Temp: _____ Air Temp: _____ Hours Fished: _____

Wind Direction: _____ Wind Speed: _____ Humidity: _____

Weather: ☀ ☁ ☔ ❄ _____

Moon Phase: _____ ◐ ◑ ● ◑ ◑ ○

Tide Details: _____

Notes: _____

_____

Fish Caught

Species	Bait	Length	Weight	Time
Other Notes:				
Other Notes:				
Other Notes:				
Other Notes:				
Other Notes:				
Other Notes:				
Other Notes:				
Other Notes:				

Fish Caught

Species	Bait	Length	Weight	Time
Other Notes:				
Other Notes:				
Other Notes:				
Other Notes:				
Other Notes:				
Other Notes:				
Other Notes:				
Other Notes:				
Other Notes:				
Other Notes:				

Other Important Notes:

_____

_____

_____

_____

_____

_____

_____

Rating Your Experience: _____ ☆ ☆ ☆ ☆ ☆

Fishing Log

Location: _____ Date: _____

Location Details: _____

_____

Companions: _____

Water Temp: _____ Air Temp: _____ Hours Fished: _____

Wind Direction: _____ Wind Speed: _____ Humidity: _____

Weather: ☀ ☁ 🌧 ❄ _____

Moon Phase: _____ ◐ ◑ ● ◑ ◐ ○

Tide Details: _____

Notes: _____

_____

Fish Caught

Species	Bait	Length	Weight	Time
Other Notes:				
Other Notes:				
Other Notes:				
Other Notes:				
Other Notes:				
Other Notes:				
Other Notes:				
Other Notes:				

Fish Caught

Species	Bait	Length	Weight	Time
Other Notes:				
Other Notes:				
Other Notes:				
Other Notes:				
Other Notes:				
Other Notes:				
Other Notes:				
Other Notes:				
Other Notes:				

Other Important Notes:

_____

_____

_____

_____

_____

_____

_____

_____

_____

Rating Your Experience: _____ ☆ ☆ ☆ ☆ ☆

Fishing Log

Location: _____ Date: _____

Location Details: _____

_____

Companions: _____

Water Temp: _____ Air Temp: _____ Hours Fished: _____

Wind Direction: _____ Wind Speed: _____ Humidity: _____

Weather: ☀ ☁ ⛆ ⛇ _____

Moon Phase: _____ ◐ ◑ ● ◑ ◐ ○

Tide Details: _____

Notes: _____

_____

Fish Caught

Species	Bait	Length	Weight	Time
Other Notes:				
Other Notes:				
Other Notes:				
Other Notes:				
Other Notes:				
Other Notes:				
Other Notes:				
Other Notes:				

Fish Caught

Species	Bait	Length	Weight	Time
Other Notes:				
Other Notes:				
Other Notes:				
Other Notes:				
Other Notes:				
Other Notes:				
Other Notes:				
Other Notes:				
Other Notes:				

Other Important Notes:

_____

_____

_____

_____

_____

_____

_____

_____

Rating Your Experience: _____ ☆ ☆ ☆ ☆ ☆

Fishing Log

Location: _____ Date: _____

Location Details: _____

_____

Companions: _____

Water Temp: _____ Air Temp: _____ Hours Fished: _____

Wind Direction: _____ Wind Speed: _____ Humidity: _____

Weather: ☀ ☁ ⛆ ❄ _____

Moon Phase: _____ ◗ ◗ ● ◖ ◖ ○

Tide Details: _____

Notes: _____

_____

Fish Caught

Species	Bait	Length	Weight	Time
Other Notes:				
Other Notes:				
Other Notes:				
Other Notes:				
Other Notes:				
Other Notes:				
Other Notes:				
Other Notes:				

Fish Caught

Species	Bait	Length	Weight	Time
Other Notes:				
Other Notes:				
Other Notes:				
Other Notes:				
Other Notes:				
Other Notes:				
Other Notes:				
Other Notes:				
Other Notes:				

Other Important Notes:

_____

_____

_____

_____

_____

_____

_____

_____

Rating Your Experience: _____ ☆ ☆ ☆ ☆ ☆

Fishing Log

Location: _____ Date: _____

Location Details: _____

_____

Companions: _____

Water Temp: _____ Air Temp: _____ Hours Fished: _____

Wind Direction: _____ Wind Speed: _____ Humidity: _____

Weather: ☀ ☁ ⛆ ❄ _____

Moon Phase: _____ ◐ ◑ ● ◐ ◑ ○

Tide Details: _____

Notes: _____

_____

Fish Caught

Species	Bait	Length	Weight	Time
Other Notes:				
Other Notes:				
Other Notes:				
Other Notes:				
Other Notes:				
Other Notes:				
Other Notes:				
Other Notes:				

Fish Caught

Species	Bait	Length	Weight	Time
Other Notes:				
Other Notes:				
Other Notes:				
Other Notes:				
Other Notes:				
Other Notes:				
Other Notes:				
Other Notes:				
Other Notes:				

Other Important Notes:

_____

_____

_____

_____

_____

_____

_____

_____

Rating Your Experience: _____ ☆ ☆ ☆ ☆ ☆

Fishing Log

Location: _____ Date: _____

Location Details: _____

_____

Companions: _____

Water Temp: _____ Air Temp: _____ Hours Fished: _____

Wind Direction: _____ Wind Speed: _____ Humidity: _____

Weather: ☀ ☁ ☔ ❄ _____

Moon Phase: _____ ◗ ◑ ● ◐ ◔ ○

Tide Details: _____

Notes: _____

_____

Fish Caught

Species	Bait	Length	Weight	Time
Other Notes:				
Other Notes:				
Other Notes:				
Other Notes:				
Other Notes:				
Other Notes:				
Other Notes:				
Other Notes:				

Fish Caught

Species	Bait	Length	Weight	Time
Other Notes:				
Other Notes:				
Other Notes:				
Other Notes:				
Other Notes:				
Other Notes:				
Other Notes:				
Other Notes:				
Other Notes:				

Other Important Notes:

_____

_____

_____

_____

_____

_____

_____

_____

Rating Your Experience: _ _____ ☆ ☆ ☆ ☆ ☆

Fishing Log

Location: _____ Date: _____

Location Details: _____

_____

Companions: _____

Water Temp: _____ Air Temp: _____ Hours Fished: _____

Wind Direction: _____ Wind Speed: _____ Humidity: _____

Weather: ☀ ☁ ☔ ❄ _____

Moon Phase: _____ ◐ ◑ ● ◑ ◐ ○

Tide Details: _____

Notes: _____

_____

Fish Caught

	Species	Bait	Length	Weight	Time
Other Notes:					
Other Notes:					
Other Notes:					
Other Notes:					
Other Notes:					
Other Notes:					
Other Notes:					
Other Notes:					

Fish Caught

Species	Bait	Length	Weight	Time
Other Notes:				
Other Notes:				
Other Notes:				
Other Notes:				
Other Notes:				
Other Notes:				
Other Notes:				
Other Notes:				
Other Notes:				

Other Important Notes:

_____

_____

_____

_____

_____

_____

_____

_____

Rating Your Experience: _____ ☆ ☆ ☆ ☆ ☆

Fishing Log

Location: _____ Date: _____

Location Details: _____

_____

Companions: _____

Water Temp: _____ Air Temp: _____ Hours Fished: _____

Wind Direction: _____ Wind Speed: _____ Humidity: _____

Weather: ☀ ☁ ☔ ❄ _____

Moon Phase: _____ ☽ ☽ ● ☾ ☾ ○

Tide Details: _____

Notes: _____

_____

Fish Caught

Species	Bait	Length	Weight	Time
Other Notes:				
Other Notes:				
Other Notes:				
Other Notes:				
Other Notes:				
Other Notes:				
Other Notes:				
Other Notes:				

Fish Caught

Species	Bait	Length	Weight	Time
Other Notes:				
Other Notes:				
Other Notes:				
Other Notes:				
Other Notes:				
Other Notes:				
Other Notes:				
Other Notes:				
Other Notes:				

Other Important Notes:

_____

_____

_____

_____

_____

_____

_____

_____

Rating Your Experience: _ _____ ☆ ☆ ☆ ☆ ☆

Fishing Log

Location: _____ Date: _____

Location Details: _____

_____

Companions: _____

Water Temp: _____ Air Temp: _____ Hours Fished: _____

Wind Direction: _____ Wind Speed: _____ Humidity: _____

Weather: ☀ ☁ ☔ ❄ _____

Moon Phase: _____ ◐ ◑ ● ◑ ◐ ○

Tide Details: _____

Notes: _____

_____

Fish Caught

Species	Bait	Length	Weight	Time
Other Notes:				
Other Notes:				
Other Notes:				
Other Notes:				
Other Notes:				
Other Notes:				
Other Notes:				
Other Notes:				

Fish Caught

Species	Bait	Length	Weight	Time
Other Notes:				
Other Notes:				
Other Notes:				
Other Notes:				
Other Notes:				
Other Notes:				
Other Notes:				
Other Notes:				
Other Notes:				

Other Important Notes:

_____

_____

_____

_____

_____

_____

_____

_____

Rating Your Experience: _ _____ ☆ ☆ ☆ ☆ ☆

Fishing Log

Location: _____ Date: _____

Location Details: _____

_____

Companions: _____

Water Temp: _____ Air Temp: _____ Hours Fished: _____

Wind Direction: _____ Wind Speed: _____ Humidity: _____

Weather: ☀ ☁ ☁🌧 ❄☁ _____

Moon Phase: _____ ◐ ◑ ● ◐ ◑ ○

Tide Details: _____

Notes: _____

_____

Fish Caught

Species	Bait	Length	Weight	Time
Other Notes:				
Other Notes:				
Other Notes:				
Other Notes:				
Other Notes:				
Other Notes:				
Other Notes:				
Other Notes:				

Fish Caught

Species	Bait	Length	Weight	Time
Other Notes:				
Other Notes:				
Other Notes:				
Other Notes:				
Other Notes:				
Other Notes:				
Other Notes:				
Other Notes:				
Other Notes:				

Other Important Notes:

_____

_____

_____

_____

_____

_____

_____

_____

Rating Your Experience: _____ ☆ ☆ ☆ ☆ ☆

Fishing Log

Location: _____ Date: _____

Location Details: _____

_____

Companions: _____

Water Temp: _____ Air Temp: _____ Hours Fished: _____

Wind Direction: _____ Wind Speed: _____ Humidity: _____

Weather: ☀ ☁ ☔ ❄ _____

Moon Phase: _____ ◐ ◑ ● ◐ ◑ ○

Tide Details: _____

Notes: _____

Fish Caught

Species	Bait	Length	Weight	Time
Other Notes:				
Other Notes:				
Other Notes:				
Other Notes:				
Other Notes:				
Other Notes:				
Other Notes:				
Other Notes:				

Fish Caught

Species	Bait	Length	Weight	Time
Other Notes:				
Other Notes:				
Other Notes:				
Other Notes:				
Other Notes:				
Other Notes:				
Other Notes:				
Other Notes:				
Other Notes:				

Other Important Notes:

_____

_____

_____

_____

_____

_____

_____

_____

Rating Your Experience: _____ ☆ ☆ ☆ ☆ ☆

Fishing Log

Location: _____ Date: _____

Location Details: _____

_____

Companions: _____

Water Temp: _____ Air Temp: _____ Hours Fished: _____

Wind Direction: _____ Wind Speed: _____ Humidity: _____

Weather: ☀ ☁ ☂ ❄ _____

Moon Phase: _____ ◑ ◑ ● ◐ ◐ ○

Tide Details: _____

Notes: _____

_____

Fish Caught

Species	Bait	Length	Weight	Time
Other Notes:				
Other Notes:				
Other Notes:				
Other Notes:				
Other Notes:				
Other Notes:				
Other Notes:				
Other Notes:				

Fish Caught

Species	Bait	Length	Weight	Time
Other Notes:				
Other Notes:				
Other Notes:				
Other Notes:				
Other Notes:				
Other Notes:				
Other Notes:				
Other Notes:				
Other Notes:				

Other Important Notes:

_____

_____

_____

_____

_____

_____

_____

_____

Rating Your Experience: _ _____ ☆ ☆ ☆ ☆ ☆

Fishing Log

Location: _____ Date: _____

Location Details: _____
_____

Companions: _____

Water Temp: _____ Air Temp: _____ Hours Fished: _____

Wind Direction: _____ Wind Speed: _____ Humidity: _____

Weather: ☀ ☁ ☔ ❄ _____

Moon Phase: _____ ◐ ◑ ● ◐ ◑ ○

Tide Details: _____

Notes: _____
_____

Fish Caught

Species	Bait	Length	Weight	Time
Other Notes:				
Other Notes:				
Other Notes:				
Other Notes:				
Other Notes:				
Other Notes:				
Other Notes:				
Other Notes:				

Fish Caught

Species	Bait	Length	Weight	Time
Other Notes:				
Other Notes:				
Other Notes:				
Other Notes:				
Other Notes:				
Other Notes:				
Other Notes:				
Other Notes:				
Other Notes:				

Other Important Notes:

_____

_____

_____

_____

_____

_____

_____

_____

Rating Your Experience: _____ ☆ ☆ ☆ ☆ ☆

Fishing Log

Location: _____ Date: _____

Location Details: _____

_____

Companions: _____

Water Temp: _____ Air Temp: _____ Hours Fished: _____

Wind Direction: _____ Wind Speed: _____ Humidity: _____

Weather: ☀ ☁ 🌧 🌨 _____

Moon Phase: _____ ◑ ◑ ● ◐ ◐ ○

Tide Details: _____

Notes: _____

_____

Fish Caught

Species	Bait	Length	Weight	Time
Other Notes:				
Other Notes:				
Other Notes:				
Other Notes:				
Other Notes:				
Other Notes:				
Other Notes:				
Other Notes:				

Fish Caught

Species	Bait	Length	Weight	Time
Other Notes:				
Other Notes:				
Other Notes:				
Other Notes:				
Other Notes:				
Other Notes:				
Other Notes:				
Other Notes:				
Other Notes:				

Other Important Notes:

_____

_____

_____

_____

_____

_____

_____

_____

Rating Your Experience: _____ ☆ ☆ ☆ ☆ ☆

Fishing Log

Location: _____ Date: _____

Location Details: _____

_____

Companions: _____

Water Temp: _____ Air Temp: _____ Hours Fished: _____

Wind Direction: _____ Wind Speed: _____ Humidity: _____

Weather: ☀ ☁ ☂ ❄ _____

Moon Phase: _____ ◑ ◑ ● ◐ ◐ ○

Tide Details: _____

Notes: _____

_____

Fish Caught

Species	Bait	Length	Weight	Time
Other Notes:				
Other Notes:				
Other Notes:				
Other Notes:				
Other Notes:				
Other Notes:				
Other Notes:				
Other Notes:				

Fish Caught

Species	Bait	Length	Weight	Time
Other Notes:				
Other Notes:				
Other Notes:				
Other Notes:				
Other Notes:				
Other Notes:				
Other Notes:				
Other Notes:				
Other Notes:				

Other Important Notes:

_____

_____

_____

_____

_____

_____

_____

_____

Rating Your Experience: _____ ☆ ☆ ☆ ☆ ☆

Fishing Log

Location: _____ Date: _____

Location Details: _____

_____

Companions: _____

Water Temp: _____ Air Temp: _____ Hours Fished: _____

Wind Direction: _____ Wind Speed: _____ Humidity: _____

Weather: ☀ ☁ ☔ ❄ _____

Moon Phase: _____ ◐ ◑ ● ◐ ◑ ○

Tide Details: _____

Notes: _____

_____

Fish Caught

Species	Bait	Length	Weight	Time
Other Notes:				
Other Notes:				
Other Notes:				
Other Notes:				
Other Notes:				
Other Notes:				
Other Notes:				
Other Notes:				

Fish Caught

Species	Bait	Length	Weight	Time
Other Notes:				
Other Notes:				
Other Notes:				
Other Notes:				
Other Notes:				
Other Notes:				
Other Notes:				
Other Notes:				
Other Notes:				
Other Notes:				

Other Important Notes:

_____

_____

_____

_____

_____

_____

_____

Rating Your Experience: _____ ☆ ☆ ☆ ☆ ☆

Fishing Log

Location: _____ Date: _____

Location Details: _____

_____

Companions: _____

Water Temp: _____ Air Temp: _____ Hours Fished: _____

Wind Direction: _____ Wind Speed: _____ Humidity: _____

Weather: ☀ ☁ ☂ ❄ _____

Moon Phase: _____ ◐ ◑ ● ◑ ◐ ○

Tide Details: _____

Notes: _____

_____

Fish Caught

Species	Bait	Length	Weight	Time
Other Notes:				
Other Notes:				
Other Notes:				
Other Notes:				
Other Notes:				
Other Notes:				
Other Notes:				
Other Notes:				

Fish Caught

Species	Bait	Length	Weight	Time
Other Notes:				
Other Notes:				
Other Notes:				
Other Notes:				
Other Notes:				
Other Notes:				
Other Notes:				
Other Notes:				
Other Notes:				

Other Important Notes:

_____

_____

_____

_____

_____

_____

_____

_____

Rating Your Experience: _ _____ ☆ ☆ ☆ ☆ ☆

Fishing Log

Location: _____ Date: _____

Location Details: _____

_____

Companions: _____

Water Temp: _____ Air Temp: _____ Hours Fished: _____

Wind Direction: _____ Wind Speed: _____ Humidity: _____

Weather: ☀ ☁ 🌧 ❄ _____

Moon Phase: _____ ◑ ◑ ● ◐ ◐ ○

Tide Details: _____

Notes: _____

_____

Fish Caught

Species	Bait	Length	Weight	Time
Other Notes:				
Other Notes:				
Other Notes:				
Other Notes:				
Other Notes:				
Other Notes:				
Other Notes:				
Other Notes:				

Fish Caught

Species	Bait	Length	Weight	Time
Other Notes:				
Other Notes:				
Other Notes:				
Other Notes:				
Other Notes:				
Other Notes:				
Other Notes:				
Other Notes:				
Other Notes:				

Other Important Notes:

_____

_____

_____

_____

_____

_____

_____

_____

Rating Your Experience: _____ ☆ ☆ ☆ ☆ ☆

Fishing Log

Location: _____ Date: _____

Location Details: _____

_____

Companions: _____

Water Temp: _____ Air Temp: _____ Hours Fished: _____

Wind Direction: _____ Wind Speed: _____ Humidity: _____

Weather: ☀ ☁ ⛆ ❄ _____

Moon Phase: _____ ◐ ◑ ● ◑ ◐ ○

Tide Details: _____

Notes: _____

_____

Fish Caught

Species	Bait	Length	Weight	Time
Other Notes:				
Other Notes:				
Other Notes:				
Other Notes:				
Other Notes:				
Other Notes:				
Other Notes:				
Other Notes:				

Fish Caught

Species	Bait	Length	Weight	Time
Other Notes:				
Other Notes:				
Other Notes:				
Other Notes:				
Other Notes:				
Other Notes:				
Other Notes:				
Other Notes:				
Other Notes:				

Other Important Notes:

_____

_____

_____

_____

_____

_____

_____

Rating Your Experience: _ _____ ☆ ☆ ☆ ☆ ☆

Fishing Log

Location: _____ Date: _____

Location Details: _____

_____

Companions: _____

Water Temp: _____ Air Temp: _____ Hours Fished: _____

Wind Direction: _____ Wind Speed: _____ Humidity: _____

Weather: ☀ ☁ ⛅ ❄ _____

Moon Phase: _____ ◐ ◑ ● ◑ ◐ ○

Tide Details: _____

Notes: _____

_____

Fish Caught

Species	Bait	Length	Weight	Time
Other Notes:
Other Notes:
Other Notes:
Other Notes:
Other Notes:
Other Notes:
Other Notes:
Other Notes:

Fish Caught

Species	Bait	Length	Weight	Time
Other Notes:				
Other Notes:				
Other Notes:				
Other Notes:				
Other Notes:				
Other Notes:				
Other Notes:				
Other Notes:				
Other Notes:				

Other Important Notes:

_____

_____

_____

_____

_____

_____

_____

_____

_____

Rating Your Experience: _____ ☆ ☆ ☆ ☆ ☆

Fishing Log

Location: _____ Date: _____

Location Details: _____

_____

Companions: _____

Water Temp: _____ Air Temp: _____ Hours Fished: _____

Wind Direction: _____ Wind Speed: _____ Humidity: _____

Weather: ☀ ☁ ☁☂ ☁❄ _____

Moon Phase: _____ ◗ ◗ ● ◖ ◖ ○

Tide Details: _____

Notes: _____

_____

Fish Caught

Species	Bait	Length	Weight	Time
Other Notes:				
Other Notes:				
Other Notes:				
Other Notes:				
Other Notes:				
Other Notes:				
Other Notes:				
Other Notes:				

Fish Caught

Species	Bait	Length	Weight	Time
Other Notes:				
Other Notes:				
Other Notes:				
Other Notes:				
Other Notes:				
Other Notes:				
Other Notes:				
Other Notes:				
Other Notes:				

Other Important Notes:

_____

_____

_____

_____

_____

_____

_____

_____

Rating Your Experience: _ _____ ☆ ☆ ☆ ☆ ☆

Fishing Log

Location: _____ Date: _____

Location Details: _____

_____

Companions: _____

Water Temp: _____ Air Temp: _____ Hours Fished: _____

Wind Direction: _____ Wind Speed: _____ Humidity: _____

Weather: ☀ ☁ ☂ ❄ _____

Moon Phase: _____ ☽ ☽ ● ☾ ☾ ○

Tide Details: _____

Notes: _____

_____

Fish Caught

Species	Bait	Length	Weight	Time
Other Notes:				
Other Notes:				
Other Notes:				
Other Notes:				
Other Notes:				
Other Notes:				
Other Notes:				
Other Notes:				

Fish Caught

Species	Bait	Length	Weight	Time
Other Notes:				
Other Notes:				
Other Notes:				
Other Notes:				
Other Notes:				
Other Notes:				
Other Notes:				
Other Notes:				
Other Notes:				

Other Important Notes:

_____

_____

_____

_____

_____

_____

_____

_____

Rating Your Experience: _ _____ ☆ ☆ ☆ ☆ ☆

Fishing Log

Location: _____ Date: _____

Location Details: _____

_____

Companions: _____

Water Temp: _____ Air Temp: _____ Hours Fished: _____

Wind Direction: _____ Wind Speed: _____ Humidity: _____

Weather: ☀ ☁ ☔ ❄ _____

Moon Phase: _____ ◐ ◐ ● ◐ ◐ ○

Tide Details: _____

Notes: _____

_____

Fish Caught

Species	Bait	Length	Weight	Time
Other Notes:				
Other Notes:				
Other Notes:				
Other Notes:				
Other Notes:				
Other Notes:				
Other Notes:				
Other Notes:				

Fish Caught

Species	Bait	Length	Weight	Time
Other Notes:				
Other Notes:				
Other Notes:				
Other Notes:				
Other Notes:				
Other Notes:				
Other Notes:				
Other Notes:				
Other Notes:				

Other Important Notes:

_____

_____

_____

_____

_____

_____

_____

_____

Rating Your Experience: _ _____ ☆ ☆ ☆ ☆ ☆

Fishing Log

Location: _____ Date: _____

Location Details: _____

_____

Companions: _____

Water Temp: _____ Air Temp: _____ Hours Fished: _____

Wind Direction: _____ Wind Speed: _____ Humidity: _____

Weather: ☀ ☁ 🌧 🌨 _____

Moon Phase: _____ ◑ ◑ ● ◐ ◐ ○

Tide Details: _____

Notes: _____

_____

Fish Caught

Species	Bait	Length	Weight	Time
Other Notes:				
Other Notes:				
Other Notes:				
Other Notes:				
Other Notes:				
Other Notes:				
Other Notes:				
Other Notes:				

Fish Caught

Species	Bait	Length	Weight	Time
Other Notes:				
Other Notes:				
Other Notes:				
Other Notes:				
Other Notes:				
Other Notes:				
Other Notes:				
Other Notes:				
Other Notes:				

Other Important Notes:

_____

_____

_____

_____

_____

_____

_____

_____

Rating Your Experience: _ _____ ☆ ☆ ☆ ☆ ☆

Fishing Log

Location: _____ Date: _____

Location Details: _____

_____

Companions: _____

Water Temp: _____ Air Temp: _____ Hours Fished: _____

Wind Direction: _____ Wind Speed: _____ Humidity: _____

Weather: ☀ ☁ 🌧 🌨 _____

Moon Phase: _____ ◐ ◑ ● ◑ ◐ ○

Tide Details: _____

Notes: _____

_____

Fish Caught

Species	Bait	Length	Weight	Time
Other Notes:				
Other Notes:				
Other Notes:				
Other Notes:				
Other Notes:				
Other Notes:				
Other Notes:				
Other Notes:				

Fish Caught

Species	Bait	Length	Weight	Time
Other Notes:				
Other Notes:				
Other Notes:				
Other Notes:				
Other Notes:				
Other Notes:				
Other Notes:				
Other Notes:				
Other Notes:				

Other Important Notes:

_____

_____

_____

_____

_____

_____

_____

_____

_____

Rating Your Experience: _ _____ ☆ ☆ ☆ ☆ ☆

Fishing Log

Location: _____ Date: _____

Location Details: _____

_____

Companions: _____

Water Temp: _____ Air Temp: _____ Hours Fished: _____

Wind Direction: _____ Wind Speed: _____ Humidity: _____

Weather: ☀ ☁ ☂ ☃ _____

Moon Phase: _____ ◗ ◗ ● ◖ ◖ ○

Tide Details: _____

Notes: _____

_____

Fish Caught

Species	Bait	Length	Weight	Time
Other Notes:				
Other Notes:				
Other Notes:				
Other Notes:				
Other Notes:				
Other Notes:				
Other Notes:				
Other Notes:				

Fish Caught

Species	Bait	Length	Weight	Time
Other Notes:				
Other Notes:				
Other Notes:				
Other Notes:				
Other Notes:				
Other Notes:				
Other Notes:				
Other Notes:				
Other Notes:				

Other Important Notes:

_____

_____

_____

_____

_____

_____

_____

_____

Rating Your Experience: _____ ☆ ☆ ☆ ☆ ☆

Fishing Log

Location: _____ Date: _____

Location Details: _____

_____

Companions: _____

Water Temp: _____ Air Temp: _____ Hours Fished: _____

Wind Direction: _____ Wind Speed: _____ Humidity: _____

Weather: ☀ ☁ 🌧 ❄ _____

Moon Phase: _____ ◗ ◑ ● ◐ ◔ ○

Tide Details: _____

Notes: _____

Fish Caught

Species	Bait	Length	Weight	Time
Other Notes:				
Other Notes:				
Other Notes:				
Other Notes:				
Other Notes:				
Other Notes:				
Other Notes:				
Other Notes:				

Fish Caught

Species	Bait	Length	Weight	Time
Other Notes:				
Other Notes:				
Other Notes:				
Other Notes:				
Other Notes:				
Other Notes:				
Other Notes:				
Other Notes:				
Other Notes:				

Other Important Notes:

_____

_____

_____

_____

_____

_____

_____

_____

_____

Rating Your Experience: _ _____ ☆ ☆ ☆ ☆ ☆

Fishing Log

Location: _____ Date: _____

Location Details: _____

_____

Companions: _____

Water Temp: _____ Air Temp: _____ Hours Fished: _____

Wind Direction: _____ Wind Speed: _____ Humidity: _____

Weather: ☀ ☁ ⛆ ❄ _____

Moon Phase: _____ ◐ ◑ ● ◑ ◐ ○

Tide Details: _____

Notes: _____

_____

Fish Caught

Species	Bait	Length	Weight	Time
Other Notes:				
Other Notes:				
Other Notes:				
Other Notes:				
Other Notes:				
Other Notes:				
Other Notes:				
Other Notes:				

Fish Caught

Species	Bait	Length	Weight	Time
Other Notes:				
Other Notes:				
Other Notes:				
Other Notes:				
Other Notes:				
Other Notes:				
Other Notes:				
Other Notes:				
Other Notes:				

Other Important Notes:

_____

_____

_____

_____

_____

_____

_____

Rating Your Experience: _____ ☆ ☆ ☆ ☆ ☆

Fishing Log

Location: _____ Date: _____

Location Details: _____

_____

Companions: _____

Water Temp: _____ Air Temp: _____ Hours Fished: _____

Wind Direction: _____ Wind Speed: _____ Humidity: _____

Weather: ☀ ☁ 🌧 🌨 _____

Moon Phase: _____ ◗ ◑ ● ◐ ◑ ○

Tide Details: _____

Notes: _____

_____

Fish Caught

Species	Bait	Length	Weight	Time
Other Notes:				
Other Notes:				
Other Notes:				
Other Notes:				
Other Notes:				
Other Notes:				
Other Notes:				
Other Notes:				

Fish Caught

Species	Bait	Length	Weight	Time
Other Notes:				
Other Notes:				
Other Notes:				
Other Notes:				
Other Notes:				
Other Notes:				
Other Notes:				
Other Notes:				
Other Notes:				

Other Important Notes:

_____

_____

_____

_____

_____

_____

_____

_____

Rating Your Experience: _ _____ ☆ ☆ ☆ ☆ ☆

Fishing Log

Location: _____ Date: _____

Location Details: _____

_____

Companions: _____

Water Temp: _____ Air Temp: _____ Hours Fished: _____

Wind Direction: _____ Wind Speed: _____ Humidity: _____

Weather: ☀ ☁ ☔ ❄ _____

Moon Phase: _____ ◗ ◑ ● ◐ ◔ ○

Tide Details: _____

Notes: _____

_____

Fish Caught

Species	Bait	Length	Weight	Time
Other Notes:				
Other Notes:				
Other Notes:				
Other Notes:				
Other Notes:				
Other Notes:				
Other Notes:				
Other Notes:				

Fish Caught

Species	Bait	Length	Weight	Time
Other Notes:				
Other Notes:				
Other Notes:				
Other Notes:				
Other Notes:				
Other Notes:				
Other Notes:				
Other Notes:				
Other Notes:				

Other Important Notes:

_____

_____

_____

_____

_____

_____

_____

_____

Rating Your Experience: _____ ☆ ☆ ☆ ☆ ☆

Fishing Log

Location: _____ Date: _____

Location Details: _____

_____

Companions: _____

Water Temp: _____ Air Temp: _____ Hours Fished: _____

Wind Direction: _____ Wind Speed: _____ Humidity: _____

Weather: ☀ ☁ ☂ ❄ _____

Moon Phase: _____ ◐ ◑ ● ◑ ◐ ○

Tide Details: _____

Notes: _____

_____

Fish Caught

Species	Bait	Length	Weight	Time
Other Notes:				
Other Notes:				
Other Notes:				
Other Notes:				
Other Notes:				
Other Notes:				
Other Notes:				
Other Notes:				

Fish Caught

Species	Bait	Length	Weight	Time
Other Notes:				
Other Notes:				
Other Notes:				
Other Notes:				
Other Notes:				
Other Notes:				
Other Notes:				
Other Notes:				
Other Notes:				

Other Important Notes:

_____

_____

_____

_____

_____

_____

_____

_____

Rating Your Experience: _____ ☆ ☆ ☆ ☆ ☆

Other Notes:

Made in the USA
Columbia, SC
29 August 2022

66311857R00061